I0540534

DO PETS GO TO HEAVEN?

A Christian Guide to Hope and Faith

JohnMark Everheart

Do Pets Go To Heaven?

Copyright 2025 by JohnMark Everheart

CONTENTS

PREFACE

Our faithful pets are police dogs, soldiers' partners in times of war, eyes for the blind, lifesavers in emergency situations, or just everyday family companions. However, there comes a time when we all must bid farewell to them. Which begs the question:

Do they go to Heaven? Do animals have a soul like mankind? These and other questions will be addressed in this book.

The loss of a cherished family pet challenges us all to dig deeper for an answer to the fundamental question, *"Where do my pets go when they die?"* Furthermore, this unique subject matter is a focus for many pet owners of all ages, from all countries and continents. You could say that being a pet owner is a universal language that establishes a common bond between people of different nationalities.

Finally, this little pet book is dedicated to

all who love and cherish the companionship of a faithful pet, bringing encouragement and comfort to all families and friends who have bid farewell to a beloved family member, "their pet".

CHAPTER 1

A DOG NAMED SPARKY BOY

*A*nyone who has enjoyed owning a pet as a valued family member can identify with the following story. The narrative begins by recalling the day we first selected our faithful pet. Then we elaborate on those special moments that we built together, with the overflowing years of blissful shared memories! Moreover, their warm personality and adorable loyalty, as well as their family spirit, are something we will never forget!-

Our story begins with a heartfelt memory of a little Pomeranian dog with a lively, cheerful personality and a ready smile. While he was a part of our lives, we will continue to have sentimental and happy memories that will keep us moving forward in life until we reunite once again!

Sparky Boy was born on a small family dairy farm in a rural area. The owners did not have the time to raise the puppy, so they gave the puppy to a friend who owned a pet shop in the city. Just one month later, Lily, a lonely businesswoman, went to the local pet market in her small town, hoping to find a special puppy for her home. When she arrived at the pet shop, Lily found the puppy wrapped warmly in a blanket. "I'm looking for a white, fluffy pup for my home," she told the shop owner.

The owner replied, smiling, "We have just what you're looking for right here."

Lily picked up the puppy and wrapped her arms around the little, ashen snowball of joy! When she said, "Sparky," Lily knew this was her boy! She never wanted to put him down, and when their eyes connected, she felt a wonderful, warm, affectionate, mirror-like image of a puppy's love in return.

Lily bought Sparky Boy, and together they headed home, where she prepared a cozy box for him in her room. She was extremely excited to share her days with Sparky Boy, who became a cherished member of the family and an important part of Lily's life.

As is life, Lily had to work every day; however, the happiest time was after work, when she rushed home to see her loving puppy. When Sparky heard the sound of the door, he ran to greet Lily with exuberance!

As with any new puppy, Sparky needed to learn where to do his business. Jokingly, Lily said, "I will give you diapers," but of course, she didn't. She began housebreaking her pup.

As spring turned to summer, Sparky Boy first learned to use puppy pads indoors and then to make his deposits outside on the ground. In time, Sparky Boy learned to eat adult dog food. He matured, and his hair grew longer. Sparky was very content just to play; he loved playing with his doggie toys, balloons, and olive-green tennis balls. His bark was filled with happiness. As with all dogs, Sparky would occasionally nibble shoes when teething. He even nibbled Lily's $200 shoes from Saks Fifth Avenue. Lily was content to wait for Sparky to grow up into a handsome, mature dog.

Winter turned to spring once again; it was Sparky Boy's first birthday. "I'll buy you a birthday cake to celebrate!" Lily told him. She helped Sparky "blow out" the candles. Sparky loved the few bites of his delicious cake and swallowed a mouthful! This was a heartfelt and gentle time for both of them.

Sparky was really a family member, an indispensable part of Lily's life. No matter where she went, it was difficult not to feel anxious to rush home to play with him and take him for a walk. Sparky was always neat and gentlemanly, and he won over a lot of people. They would say, "What a handsome boy!"

Now, most pet owners realize that we sometimes make poor choices when disciplining our pets.

Well, Lily over-disciplined little Sparky Boy when he made a mistake. "I'll hit your butt with a shoe," Lily said. Little Sparky yelped and wanted to escape from this hurt. Then, Lily realized her actions were wrong and became deeply sorrowful and regretful for striking Sparky. She just wanted to teach him not to poop everywhere in the house, and that he should not jump on her bed when she was not there. Lily realized that she should not hit Sparky, that he was so young and small that sometimes he could not control himself. Lily was very sorry. Even though Sparky was punished, he never held a grudge. Sparky was always so happy and was constantly ready to lick Lily's hand, to sleep in her shoes, and to comfort her when she was sad.

One day, Lily encountered the most difficult and painful day of her life. Her marriage had come to an end, and she was unable to attend to Sparky. She left him alone all day at home. Sparky took care of himself, eating and drinking. When Lily arrived home from work and rested on the sofa, Sparky lay quietly beside her, watching her cry and licking her tears to comfort her.

After some time had passed, Lily's pain diminished. As she became stronger in spirit, Lily felt better. Once again, she took Sparky Boy for long walks, and he would meet many new dog friends. From the high-rise apartment window, Sparky would look down through the balcony, eager to see the shadows of his friends, and then he would beg Lily to take him out.

One bright summer day, Lily wanted to teach Sparky how to swim at one of their favorite spots, Swan Fountain Lake. Excited, Sparky Boy worked hard to doggy paddle, causing Lily to laugh aloud. However, Lily soon realized, because of the panic in Sparky's eyes, that he was terrified of the water. Another day, at Swan Fountain Lake, Sparky was on the other side of the lake when Lily called him. He did not hesitate to jump into the water, desperately swimming across the lake to her without any fear! It was then that Lily realized the special place she had in his little heart. Sparky loved Lily and would do anything to protect her and keep her safe!

Lily lived alone in her high-rise apartment for several years. Then, one year later, Lily met a wonderful, kind man named Chris, who developed a deep and abiding affection for not only Lily but also Sparky Boy. He treasured Sparky very much, and he never let Lily over-discipline him.

No matter what happened or how difficult a situation was, Sparky was always with them, quietly licking their hands and providing his unconditional love. When it was cold outside, he would lie on their feet and give them the warmth of his fluffy, white fur. When they returned home from a hard day's work, Sparky Boy greeted Chris and Lily with his own joyful dance to welcome them as they opened the front door. Lily knew her place as the caregiver was to provide the home, and the small but loving Sparky knew he must wait for her return. Lily's dream was to give Sparky a big, warm house so he could enjoy the complete freedom of playing in a backyard and enjoying the rest of his years in a place called "home."

The Seventh Year

In Sparky Boy's seventh year, Lily and Chris moved from city life to the warm and sandy beaches along the coast. However, they were both concerned and uneasy about the move.

9

This was the first time he would be traveling on an airplane, and they were very worried about his safety. They prayed to God for his protection and a safe and sound arrival. When they received a call that the plane had landed, Lily and Chris went to the airport to pick up Sparky Boy. They found him lying very quietly and extremely sad in a carrier crate. As they stepped closer to his crate, Sparky heard their voices calling his name; he jumped up immediately and replied with a hoarse yet excited bark, scratching at the sides of his carrier crate. They knew Sparky was trying to tell them, loudly, how hard this day of separation had been for his little, precious spirit. Then Lily and Chris happily called, *"Sparky Boy, we care for you! We will not leave or abandon you!"*

As fast as possible, Lily and Chris released Sparky Boy from his crate. He quivered with gladness and then jumped into their arms with excitement! They patted him repeatedly and enjoyed the warm hugs, happy to feel Sparky Boy's licks as they were reunited! Oh, what a happy day that was for all of them! Lily and Chris were thankful to God that their precious, furry cargo had arrived without a scratch!

The next day, Sparky Boy cheerfully walked on the beach with Lily and Chris. He loved the beautiful beach and warm sunshine. His little paws painted colors of joy on the beach as he left his paw prints behind. When they let go of his leash and he was able to jog freely, Sparky Boy would not run away; instead, he would run around both of them, creating a chain of overlapping circles in the sand while they walked forward. Both Lily and Chris were puzzled by this unique behavior. However, they believed Sparky was declaring to one and all, "These are my owners! This is my warm family! I'm glad to be with them, walking on the sandy seashore!"

Several times, Lily and Chris took Sparky Boy into the ocean to teach him to swim, but he remained afraid of water, always trying desperately to get back to shore. However, Sparky Boy always heard their comforting words in his ears: "*Sparky Boy, Mommy and Daddy are here. Do not be afraid; we will keep you from harm.*"

Sparky Boy built up his courage a few steps at a time. Finally, he learned to swim in the ocean. Lily and Chris saw his progress and rewarded him with big hugs and encouraging words. Sparky happily wagged his tail, always wanting to please them. When Lily and Chris held their lovable dog about ten inches above the water, he always began to "air paddle." Lily and Chris laughed every time!

With the passage of time, Sparky grew into a

very handsome adult dog. His small ears were always alert; his eyes, set off by long eyelashes, were always wide open and shining like the sun, and his mouth always showed a bright smile! His pink tongue often slipped over his outer lip, making it look like he was about to find good food to eat. When he was outside, he was always preoccupied with looking for his owners, always eager to play and keep Lily and Chris company.

In places like the sandy beach, where there was no risk of cars, Lily and Chris could let go of the leash, and he could run as free as an eagle. Sometimes, Sparky Boy didn't listen to Lily and Chris's gentle warnings; he was too excited to see other dogs and was eager to run and play, unaware of the potential dangers posed by other dogs that might bite him. Because Sparky was so trusting and had a good-hearted nature, he just wanted to show other people and other dogs his friendly, warm, and gentle spirit! All Sparky Boy desired to do was share his unconditional friendship, even to the point of endangering his own well-being and safety. Every time this happened, Lily desperately ran to be by his side and protect him from harm. When Sparky was obedient, he enjoyed the loving hugs Lily and Chris gave him, as well as the favorite foods they prepared for him as a reward.

When Lily and Chris had a meal of assorted meats, chicken, and fish, Sparky always insisted on the first bite. He'd stare at Lily and Chris with big, brown, eager eyes so that they would see his expression of disappointment, which would remain until they gave him a taste. However, there were times when Lily did not share her food; Sparky was such a kind-hearted dog that he never showed resentment or held a grudge.

When people asked Sparky Boy's age, Lily would say, "Almost eight years old!" Then they would reply, "Your dog is old." Lily always corrected them – her Sparky Boy was young! However, Sparky Boy *was* growing old. Soon, after just an hour of play and walking, his energy began to decrease. More often than not, after a walk or playtime, Sparky would quietly and peacefully retreat into his room to sleep.

13

One day, about two months away from Sparky Boy's eighth birthday, Lily came home, and Chris told her that Sparky Boy seemed to be mildly weak and sluggish. They thought that, as with times past, Sparky Boy would feel better in a few days. In fact, Lily and Chris did not know that a deadly infection had begun to seize Sparky Boy's life. Still, after a few days, his spirit began to improve, and Sparky Boy once again began to eat and jump. They thought he was all right. In fact, the disease had worsened.

Chris had to travel overseas, and Lily took care of Sparky Boy. He ate very little, and Lily thought Sparky Boy had a cold. She bought some medicine to give him. She took him for a walk on the beach, and Sparky was happy, still looking for other dog friends. Lily and Sparky sat on a rock, watching the ocean waves and enjoying the warm sunset. They slowly walked back home when it grew dark, and Sparky was happy and joyful. However, Sparky Boy's appetite decreased. He lost his spirit and energy. Because Lily thought his loss of appetite was due to a cold, she tried to make him eat his favorites – chicken soup and ham – but still Sparky did not eat. He slept more, most often on Lily's feet, and often looked up at her sadly.

Lily saw Sparky looking at her and quickly

picked him up in her arms. "What's wrong?" she asked him. "Your eyes are so sad and longing. I can tell your heart hurts, but you are speechless. You look for your father at home, and I know you are missing him." Lily told Sparky that his father would be back in a few weeks. She gave Sparky his father's pillow to sleep on, hoping that would help. However, she sensed the incredible pain in Sparky Boy's tender, little heart and made an effort to provide additional comfort. She tried to make Sparky Boy feel better, but nothing seemed to work.

She decided it was time to have Sparky examined to find out what was wrong. Lily took Sparky Boy to the animal hospital, where the doctor told her that Sparky was in critical condition. Lily was crushed and began to cry. She had not thought Sparky was so sick. She was willing to give up all her money for his medical treatment as long as they could make him better!

The doctors were not sure they could make Sparky Boy better, but they tried. As long as there was a little hope, Lily knew they would try to save him. The doctor devised a treatment program and began injecting therapeutic antibiotics. From beginning to end, Sparky Boy rested quietly under the doctor's hands and did not cry or complain. Still, Sparky gazed sadly at Lily. She hastened to say, "Don't worry, Sparky Boy. I will not leave you here!"

Lily took Sparky Boy home. Sparky knew he was going to die, but it seemed like he was doing everything possible to stay alive. He looked at Lily with sad, tearful eyes. All the while, Lily held Sparky in her arms. She caressed his frail body while Sparky looked longingly at the door, expecting to see his father walk in. However, he could not come. Lily cradled Sparky in her arms and wept. Then Sparky Boy's ears drooped. Lily knew he fought with death, and she cried and called his name. She knew Sparky tried desperately to stay by her side, waiting for his father to come back, but he was so weak, so incredibly weak.

Just after 8:00 p.m. one Monday in March, Sparky Boy could no longer keep his eyes open. He whimpered in pain while Lily lay by his side, stroking him and whispering to him. Sparky didn't want to go. He wanted to stay! Lily called his name repeatedly, but death was pulling him away. Then Sparky, still unwilling to leave his Lily and Chris, forlornly breathed his last breath. Lily held him tight and cried in deep, grievous pain. Lily's world was now exceedingly dark without Sparky Boy!

<u>Sparky Boy's Prayer</u>

Mom and Dad, I'm gone. Please forgive me that I cannot stay with you and go to the beach. I've gone to heaven, with the freedom to have fun and fellowship with my Creator, who gave me to you! I thank Him for the time I had with both of you!

There is no disease here, no hunger, no risk of car accidents, and no risk of bullying by bigger dogs. Heaven is filled with sunshine, clean air, flowers, laughter, and so many of my friends! I will be waiting here for you both! We will reunite once again, forever, by the grace of God!

After returning home, Lily Skyped with Chris on the internet and told him the heartbreaking news. He also cried. While on his business trip, he had purchased some of Sparky Boy's favorite snacks to bring back to him. Chris was very sad. Sparky could no longer enjoy his favorite treats. He could no longer lick Chris's hand.

Chris knew that Lily was heartbroken and cried often. Day and night, filled with sweet memories of Sparky Boy, Chris and Lily remembered the energy of his high-spirited liveliness. They wanted to listen to Sparky Boy's bark again, to hold him in their arms again, but they understood that they could only hug him in heaven. In the minds of others who may not understand, Sparky Boy was "just a dog," but for Chris and Lily, Sparky Boy was a treasured member of their family for almost eight years.

Chris returned home on a Saturday, seven days after Sparky Boy had left them. It had been clear and sunny all day, but that night it began to rain. The heavens also cried for their loss.

Lily wept and snipped a little clump of Sparky Boy's ashen fur as a final memorial. They buried Sparky Boy at the beach, for he had loved the expanse of the sand and the freedom of the birds. They buried him with his favorite snacks and toys. He slept there quietly and could no longer follow them home. However, many dogs were running and playing, and Chris and Lily knew that Sparky Boy wouldn't be lonely. They visited him every day, knowing he was happy now.

To this end, we earnestly pray and ask God to let you be happy in heaven, and there, you wait for us! In heaven, playing joyfully, knowing you are in the Father's kingdom. We will play together once again in the Father's eternal park! We will meet you with our God, your Creator, in the glory of life eternal!

18

CHAPTER 2

PET STORIES

A Bird Named "Cher Ami"

Our next story begins with an unlikely pet we all take for granted – birds of the air! Our Father God tells us in Matthew 10:29 that *He is completely aware when one sparrow falls to the earth.* How much more valued are we?

In this story, we will go back in time to World War I. In those times, cell phones, satellite phones, social media, video conferencing, and other modern forms of communication had not yet been invented. Messages were sometimes transmitted by wire (telegraph or field phone during wartime). However, during wartime, a form of communication that was paramount was the carrier pigeon. When a military unit was ordered to attack over a broad and often challenging wooded landscape or densely hazardous terrain that made it impossible to string communication wires for sending and receiving information, a field commander usually carried with him several carrier pigeons.

Pigeons served numerous purposes during World War I and World War II. They were outfitted with cameras that took pictures of strategic enemy positions. But one of the most critical roles pigeons served was as messengers during wartime. An important memo would be written on a small piece of paper. Then that paper would be neatly folded and secured in a small, metal canister attached to a pigeon's leg. Once the pigeon was released, it would fly back to its home base. When it arrived, a bell or buzzer would sound, signaling its arrival to the Army officer who was on duty. The message would be read and transmitted to the proper military personnel.

In 1917, during World War I, the U.S. Army Corps was given 600 pigeons for the purpose of passing messages when it was not possible to do so by signal flag or field phone. The pigeons were donated by bird breeders in Great Britain and then trained for their jobs by American soldiers.

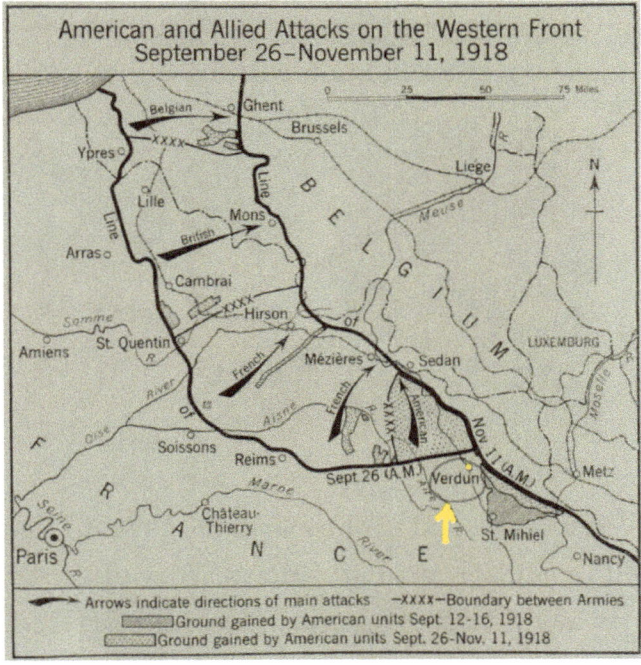

American and Allied Attacks on the Western Front September 26–November 11, 1918

During the Meuse-Argonne Offensive in France, a two-month battle that ultimately ended World War I, 442 pigeons were deployed in the Verdun, France, area to carry hundreds of critical communications. This is how the carrier pigeon system worked:

When a commander in the field needed to send a message, he first wrote it out on paper, trying to be as brief and yet as detailed as possible. Then, he called for one of his Signal Corps officers, who was in charge of the pigeons. The officer would select one of the pigeons that the soldiers had brought into combat with them. The message would be put in the canister on the bird's leg, and then the bird would be tossed high into the air to fly back to its home base behind the battle lines.

When it landed in the coop, wires would sound a bell or buzzer, and another soldier of the Signal Corps would know a message had arrived. He would go to the coop, remove the message from the canister, and then send it by telegraph, field phone, or personal messenger to the correct personnel.

Carrier pigeons had a critical job. It was also dreadfully dangerous. If the enemy soldiers were nearby when a pigeon was released, they knew that the bird would be carrying secret and significant messages. They would try their best to shoot the pigeon down so the communication couldn't be delivered. Some of these pigeons became rather famous among the infantrymen they worked for.

One pigeon named "The Mocker" flew 52 missions before he was wounded. Another was named "President Wilson." He was injured in the last week of World War I. During his mission, the enemy shot off the little pigeon's foot. Amazingly, he still delivered the message, thereby saving a large group of American infantrymen.

"Dear Friend"

Probably the most famous of all the carrier pigeons was one named "Cher Ami" (sounds like "Sherry"), two French words meaning *Dear Friend*." Cher Ami served several long months on the front lines during the fall of 1918. He flew twelve important missions to deliver messages. Perhaps the most important was the message he carried on October 4, 1918. Mr. Charles Whittlesey was a lawyer in New York, but when the United States called for soldiers to help France regain its freedom against German oppression, Whittlesey joined the Army and went to Europe to assist. He was promoted to the rank of major of a battalion of soldiers in the 77th Infantry Division, known as "The Liberty Division" because the majority of the men came from New York and wore a bright-blue patch on their shoulders that featured the Statue of Liberty.

On October 3, 1918, while engaged in battle, Major Whittlesey and more than 500 men were trapped in a small terrain depression on the side of a hill. Surrounded by enemy soldiers, many were killed and wounded on the first day.

By the second day of battle, barely 200 men were still alive, though many were injured. They prayed to God that they would be delivered from the enemy's brutal assault. Major Whittlesey sent several pigeons with a message to inform his commander-in-chief, located several miles behind the battle line, about how the enemy's calamitous ambush had compromised the battalion's position and that they needed help.

Tragically, the pigeons were being shot down by enemy guns, so they never reached the commander-in-chief with Major Whittlesey's message. By the next day, he had only one pigeon left – Cher Ami!

During the afternoon, the American artillery tried to send some protection by firing hundreds of huge rounds into the ravine where the Germans surrounded both U.S. and French regiments. Unfortunately, the American commanders did not know exactly where the American soldiers were and started dropping the big shells right on top of them. It was a horrifying situation that might have resulted in Allied forces being killed by friendly fire. Major Whittlesey called for his last pigeon, Cher Ami. The note put in the canister on his left leg read:

"We are along the road parallel to 276.4. Our own artillery is dropping a barrage directly on us. For heaven's sake, stop it."

As Cher Ami began flying back home from the front lines, the Germans saw him rising out of the thick brush and opened fire. For several minutes, bullets zipped through the air all around the petite pigeon. It looked like Cher Ami wasn't going to make through the enemy line of pistol fire and was going to plunge headlong to the ground instead. The doomed American infantrymen's spirits were crushed; their last hope of life and to return home to their families was plummeting to earth from a very heavy attack of enemy fire.

By God's grace, Cher Ami managed to spread his humble wings and flew from the tangled undergrowth, rising back into the air with all his strength and might, climbing higher and higher, until he was out of range of the enemy's guns.

This little, humble bird flew 25 incredible miles in only 25 minutes to deliver his message. Cher Ami was severely wounded by the time he finally reached his coop. He could fly no longer, and the soldier who answered the sound of the bell when Cher Ami entered the coop found the little bird lying on his back, covered in blood. He had been blinded in one eye, and a bullet had hit his breastbone, making a hole the size of a quarter. Hanging by just a few tendons was the nearly severed leg of the brave little bird. Attached to that leg was a silver canister with the all-important message from the front line.

Once the commander received the message, he immediately stopped the artillery fire, and more than 200 American lives were saved...all because that little bird would never give up trying to carry his note back home.

Cher Ami, or "Dear Friend," became the hero of the 77th Infantry Division. The French and American soldiers advocated for all to know and honor the true story of the little bird's bravery and determination. Their petition found support in the French government, which bestowed one of its greatest honors on Cher Ami. The brave carrier pigeon was presented with a medal, the *Croix de Guerre* ("War Cross") with a palm leaf.

This War Cross was a French military decoration created in 1915 and 1939 to reward extraordinary feats of bravery, either by individuals or groups, in the course of the two World Wars.

Once the men of the 77th Infantry Division discovered the condition of the little bird that had saved 200 of their friends, they were determined to carve a small, wooden leg for Cher Ami since his natural leg couldn't be saved. When he was well enough to travel, the little, one-legged hero was put on a boat to the United States of America. The commander of the entire United States Army, General John J. Pershing, personally ensured Cher Ami left port safely before they departed France.

Back in the United States, the story of Cher Ami was told over and over again. The little bird was in newspapers and magazines, and it seemed that everyone knew his name. He became one of the most famous heroes of World War I. Sadly, Cher Ami died of his multiple war wounds on June 13, 1919 – less than a year after he had completed his service to the United States Army Signal Corps.

***

What a heartwarming story of a pigeon's loyalty and dedication to duty, giving us all hope amidst life-threatening conflicts. In addition, it's wonderful to observe the unity between different nationalities as they come together to publicize and recognize the heroic efforts of a brave pigeon named Cher Ami.

God has a great concern for all His creation – both man and animal – but He cares about you as an individual the most. Let us read God's Word and discover how special and precious you are to Him!

28

Psalms 139:1-13 [1]*You have searched me, Lord, and you know me. You know when I sit and when I rise; you perceive my thoughts from afar. You discern my going out and my lying down; you are familiar with all my ways. Before a word is on my tongue you, Lord, know it completely. You hem me in behind and before, and you lay your hand upon me. Such knowledge is too wonderful for me, too lofty for me to attain.*

[7]*Where can I go from your Spirit? Where can I flee from your presence? If I go up to the heavens, you are there; if I make my bed in the depths, you are there. If I rise on the wings of the dawn, if I settle on the far side of the sea, even there your hand will guide me, your right hand will hold me fast. If I say, "Surely the darkness will hide me and the light become night around me," even the darkness will not be dark to you; the night will shine like the day, for darkness is as light to you.*

[13]*For you created my inmost being; you knit me together in my mother's womb. I praise you because I am fearfully and wonderfully made; your works are wonderful...*

Dogs of War

This next section presents a brief narrative about our pets' loyalty and protective characteristics, both past and present.

Throughout the centuries, mankind has been engaged in war. Historically, dogs have been directly or indirectly on the leading edge of the battlefield. Moreover, dogs have contributed bravely, courageously, and, I might add, faithfully on the front lines, whether officially trained to do so or motivated by loyalty to their master, the soldier.

During my research about war dogs, I discovered that the ancient Corinthians used certain large breeds of dogs with success against the Greek military legions. The Romans used dogs to guard their military and raise security alarms, as did Attila the Hun, who placed them around his camps for added protection.

Beginning with the Revolutionary War and continuing through World War I, dogs had a largely unofficial presence alongside American soldiers, often accompanying them to combat as a general's beloved pet, a mascot, or as a stray that became a companion to an obliging soldier. It wasn't until the onset of World War II that the U.S. War Department, emulating successful war dog programs in Europe, finally set into motion the military dog program that would develop (and lapse and evolve again) over the next several decades. Continuing throughout the Korean and Vietnam Wars, the Military Working Dog Program today deploys dogs to Iraq and Afghanistan.

We will take a look at one of the many thousands of war dogs whose stories are powerful testaments of the essential roles they played in saving lives and lifting spirits. Ernest Harold Baynes, a reporter who documented the use of animals during World War I, wrote, *"The fame of the war dogs may well rest on the heroic and brave work they actually did in the line of duty!"*

Duties of War Dogs

This is an overview of war dogs, how they were trained, and their service in the following areas:

Sentry dogs were trained to give warning by growling, alerting, or barking. They were especially valuable when working in the dark, as attacks from cover or the rear were most likely. Sentry dogs would also accompany a military or civilian guard on patrol and give warning of the approach or presence of strangers within the area protected.

Scout or patrol dogs: In addition to possessing the skills listed for sentry dogs, scout dogs were trained to operate in silence, aiding in the detection of snipers, ambushers, and other enemy forces.

Messenger dogs: They learned to travel silently and utilize natural cover when moving between two handlers.

Mine dogs: These dogs were trained to find trip wires, booby traps, and metallic and non-metallic land mines.

Combat tracker dogs: Using both visual clues and scents, including blood and body odors, these dogs were used to locate missing personnel, such as downed pilots, or capture enemy soldiers.[1]

A Dog Named Bruiser

The time is during one of the most senseless wars in history. Near Da Nang, Vietnam, a soldier and his war dog, a German Shepherd named Bruiser, creep forward silently in enemy territory, searching for any sign that the adversary is close. Bruiser's ears perk up, and he suddenly stops dead in his tracks, his nose up and ears twitching, indicating danger is imminent. His handler, Sergeant John Flannelly, decides to fire at the enemy. Seconds later, enemy mortar rockets, grenades, and automatic weapons fire pour down on them like heavy rain.

---

1 U.S. Army Quartermaster Museum, Fort Lee, Va.; United States War Dogs Association.

Sergeant Flannelly is lying on the ground, helpless and gravely wounded. Most of his left torso is now a wide-open gash. Sergeant Flannelly orders Bruiser to leave the battlefield, but Bruiser refuses to obey his command. He dashes to Sergeant Flannelly, opens his jaws, and grabs his shirt. The big German Shepherd hunkers down beside him and begins pulling his master to safety.

The 85 lb. dog dragged him about three hundred yards to a mortar crater hole. Then Sergeant Flannelly was medevacked to a field infirmary!

Other brave soldiers died that day, yet with Bruiser's advanced warning, many soldiers stayed alive, including Sergeant Flannelly.

Following his surgery, he immediately requested that his faithful friend, Bruiser, be by his bedside during his recovery. The staff sent word to locate Bruiser. Once found, he climbed on the bed, put his head on Sergeant Flannelly's shoulder, and affectionately licked his face. Sergeant Flannelly just held him and cried. "What do you say to someone who's saved your life?" asked the Marine.

Sergeant Flannelly, during his recovery process, reflected on the horrific event and said, "Bruiser saved not only my life but the lives of the other U.S. Marines I was working with. I never would have made it without him. I will never be able to thank him enough. I owe my life to that dog."

A Special Segment about War Dogs

Bruiser was among more than 4,000 dogs recruited to serve and protect U.S. troops in Vietnam, preventing 10,000-plus American casualties in the process in active war conditions. Yet, only a few of these dogs returned to America at the end of the war. Since these canine heroes were classified by the military as equipment, they were declared "surplus armaments" and either unceremoniously euthanized or left to unknown fates in Vietnam.

None of the dogs, however, had ever been honored for their bravery and service – until more than 21 years ago. This long-deserved recognition came through a compelling documentary called *War Dogs: America's Forgotten Heroes*, narrated by the acclaimed actor Martin Sheen.

"There would be a whole lot more than fifty thousand casualties on the Vietnam Wall memorial without these dogs ... and I don't think the average American even knows the role these dogs played," said Dr. John Kubisz, a veterinarian who served with the 764th Veterinary Detachment in Vietnam.

While *War Dogs* tells the untold story of the heroic roles played by thousands of war dogs in Vietnam, the documentary was produced primarily to educate America about the unwavering bond between dog and handler that prevented more than 10,000 casualties in Vietnam and reveal how the heroic efforts of these loyal dogs were never honored. Shedding light on the roles war dogs played presents an entirely different perspective on the Vietnam War.

"Fewer than two hundred of them ever returned home," says Dr. Kubisz. "Some three hundred twenty-five died in the line of duty, while another approximately six hundred succumbed to tropical disease. But at the end of the war, the rest were considered military equipment and were either euthanized or left behind. They deserve to be remembered."

The War Dog Memorial at Hartsdale Pet Cemetery in Hartsdale, New York, is one of only a handful of such monuments nationwide, most of which are located on military bases.

I believe these dogs of war should be recognized. Their stories serve as a poignant reminder of loyalty and affection. Many of the handlers (soldiers) say that if it weren't for their dogs, they wouldn't be alive today.

Our pets play a vital role in our lives, inspiring

unwavering devotion to us. In times of crisis, that devotion may drive them to lifesaving measures! This begs the question, *why does a dog even think about saving their owner?* How do they know their owner is in impending danger? We will answer these questions in the following chapters.

<u>What about Dolphins?</u>

If you have ever been to Sea World, Florida, you would have had an opportunity to interact with these God-created creatures! They are amazing! At the dolphin pool, you can reach out your hand to caress their skin, which is incredibly soft and warm. It is a strange experience at first, but then it becomes a completely amazing one. Wow! I'm actually petting a dolphin! Cool!

Let us explore some short but astonishing stories about dolphins saving other living beings.

Real-Life Case I: Dolphins Save Helpless Dog!

It was a humid mid-August afternoon on Marco Island, Florida. An eight-month-old, brown-and-white Labrador Retriever named "Turbo" was digging in the yard and playing with his favorite chew ball. When Cindy Burnett, one of his owners, heard the phone ring from inside the house, she laid her gardening tools down on the carpet-like grass and went to answer the call. While she was busy talking on the phone, the little pup managed to slide under the plastic fencing and escape the yard.

The home was situated on a canal and featured a boat dock. During high tide, the dog had clumsily fallen over the edge of a concrete wall and into the water. The concrete wall was too high for the pup to reach; therefore, he had no chance of getting back up on the boat dock by himself. With the wind and the current carrying him slowly along the canal and toward the deeper waters of the Gulf of Mexico, the pup needed a miracle. Ms. Cindy finished her 20-minute phone conversation. Walking to the backyard, she noticed that her pup was missing. She called his name repeatedly, but did not receive any reply, such as a bark or cry. She asked her son, Dave, if he had the dog, but he said he had not seen Turbo. Frantically, she and her son searched the street and the boat dock. They searched and searched, calling his name. Ms. Cindy drove through the area, searching for many hours, but she couldn't find her precious puppy!

In the canal, the pup had been swimming for several hours and had become exhausted as he was headed farther down the canal.

Amazingly, a pod of dolphins was in the canal. They saw Turbo and seemed to understand his dire plight. The dolphins began squealing, splashing, jumping, and even swimming close to the sandy shoreline, placing themselves at risk. It seemed they were trying to attract the attention of a group of people on the beach nearby, which, astonishingly, **seemed to be** their motive! The people saw the stranded dog and realized they could rescue him!

One of the people whose attention was captured by the noisy, demonstrative dolphins said, "They were really putting up a ruckus, almost beaching themselves on the sandbar trying to get our attention!"

Once they saw the pup, he was safely pulled out of the water by fire department personnel and reunited with his owner. It seems this little pup might have been lost for good if it weren't for a bit of help from his ocean-dwelling friends!

Ms. Cindy was filled with joy and gladness. She said, "If it wasn't for the pod of dolphins, I would have never seen the dog again." She added, "If the dolphins hadn't persisted with their splashing and strange behavior enough to get the communities' attention, the dog would have perished in the canal."

Real-Life Case II: Dolphins Saving Humans

If you have ever seen the old, classic TV show "Flipper," you have seen dolphins rescuing humans from drowning or protecting them from sharks. But does it really happen? The answer is, surprisingly, yes, it does! Here is a true story about a pod of dolphins doing just that!

On a bright, sunny morning, November 8, 2007, John hangs up the phone after talking with his girlfriend about having an awesome time at a church concert. He jumps in his Jeep Sahara at 9:03 in the morning, drives to the sandy Northern California coastline, and arrives at 9:57 a.m.

Just before 11 a.m., John is surfing in the Pacific Ocean off the coast of Monterey, California. A great white shark, estimated at 12 to 15 feet long, swam up and bumped John as he sat on his

41

surfboard. Shortly after, the shark swam toward John again. This time, its massive jaws opened and then clamped down on his torso.

That attack shredded his back, literally peeling the skin off, John explained, describing it as "like peeling a banana." But because John's stomach was pressed against the surfboard, his entrails and internal organs were protected from the shark's teeth.

The shark released John from its mouth and swam away. You would have thought that the danger was over now, right? But then the shark approached John for a third time! The shark attempted to swallow John's right leg. This was actually a good thing because the shark's grip anchored John on his surfboard while he kicked the white-toothed beast in the head and snout with his left leg until it let go.

Now, unknown to John, there was a pod of bottlenose dolphins nearby that had been horsing around in the surf while John had been under attack. Amazingly, this pod of dolphins intervened in the attack by forming a protective ring around John, allowing him to slowly swim back to shore safely.

As he got closer to shore, paramedics eagerly waded through the water to administer first aid.

"Truly a miracle, thanks to God," said John.

Our Fine, Finned Friends

Aquatic experts and the scientific community are bewildered and unable to identify why dolphins protect humans. Nevertheless, stories of these marine mammals rescuing humans go back to the ancient Grecian Empire, according to the Whale and Dolphin Conservation Society.

Why do dolphins feel the compulsion to save anyone, whether it be a man or woman or even that little puppy? In my opinion, dolphins possess a soul-like structure. Why do I say this? Only a soul-filled entity can "act out" (a psychological term for a certain behavior) to save another soul-filled entity, such as mankind! We will explore this subject further in the following chapters.

Again, I ask, *why would dolphins try to save*

another being's life? There is nothing in it for them, right? They will not receive free money, a new Jeep Wrangler Sahara, a new, colonial-style home, an ego-boosting 15 seconds of fame on Newsmax, Fox News, or CNN, or free sardines. It makes one wonder who created the dolphin to act out in such a marvelous way to save another form of life?

CHAPTER 3

HAVE YOU EVER LOST A PET?

*T*hese stories were based on actual events, and more than likely, they are very similar to your own interactions with your pet! Which leads us to our next line of thought: have you ever lost a pet? If so, we pray you have or will find the Lord's comfort. Know assuredly that one day, you will see your precious pet once again. The Lord loves you exceedingly, and He truly cares about you on a very personal level.

God has shown through His Word that animals are an important part of His creation. The playfulness, love, and devotion in our pets communicate the artistic beauty and grace of God, their Creator!

God uses pets to help us learn about lovingkindness and responsibility in caring for another precious life. From pets, we gain knowledge of mercy, compassion, and patience, along with an understanding of the power of those virtues. We also discover what it means to receive unconditional love.

Our pets offer us companionship, devotion, amusement, and joyful delight! God meant for these friends to add pleasure and fulfillment to our lives. Animals are one of every *good gift... [that] cometh down from the Father of lights* (James 1:17). God loves to give good things to us!

God Cares

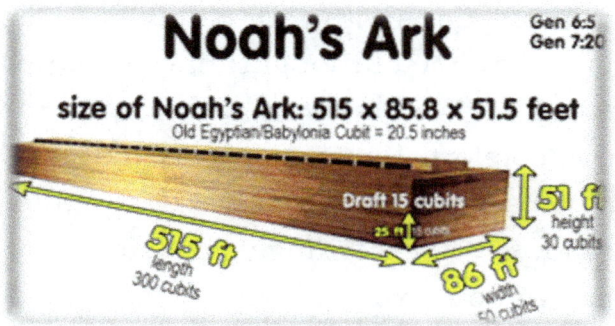

Did you ever watch the movie *Evan Almighty*? This is a short rundown of the movie plot:

Former local television news anchor and newly elected congressman, Evan Baxter (played by Steve Carell), leaves his hometown of Buffalo, New York, and relocates his family to the fictional town of Prestige Crest, Virginia, with a campaign promise to "change the world." His family is happy but concerned about the relocation.

Evan's wife, Joan (played by Lauren Graham), prays that they will grow closer as a family. Evan also prays to God to help him change the world. So far, things are going quite well for Evan; however, at the crack of dawn, weird things start to happen around him:

His alarm clock repeatedly rings at 6:14 a.m., despite being set for 7:00 a.m.

Large quantities of ancient biblical carpenter tools and wood are delivered via USPS to his house without rationalization.

Pairs of animals, dogs, cats, and birds, follow him without any apparent reason.

The digits 614 follow him everywhere he goes, whether at work, home, or while driving. He soon discovers that the set of integers 614 refers to a Bible verse in the Book of Genesis, where God instructed Noah to build an ark in preparation for a flood to save both man and animals. God (played by Morgan Freeman) appears to Evan and cordially insists that Evan construct an ark. Although Evan vehemently resists building the ark, God creates various situations, using both comedic and heartfelt events that eventually convince Evan to build the ark. Subsequently, building the ark reminds him that this is his one and only opportunity *"to change the world"* and save his community.

Finally, at the conclusion of the movie, God tells Evan that he and his family now have everything they had initially prayed for. He also tells Evan that the way to *"change the world"* is by doing one act of random kindness (ARK) at a time.

Anyway, this was a wholesome, family comedy, and it reminds me of Father God's kindness and merciful concern for all His creation, both humans and animals!

Yes, believe it or not, Father God is concerned about animals. Although an estimated 94 percent of Scripture outlines God's plan for humanity, God also makes it quite obvious that He is personally mindful of the animals, too.

Do you remember the story of Noah and the ark? If all God had cared about was saving Noah and his family, why did he tell Noah to build a boat big enough to take all those animals with him? Why did God communicate with the animals and guide them to Noah? (How did they know it was going to rain? Father God seemed to inform them in their spirit!)

We can observe clearly from this story that God wanted to save the animals. Therefore, He told Noah to construct a massive cargo ship big enough to transport and save the animals with him. We may surmise that the immensity of the ship would have allowed sufficient room for additional men and women if they had chosen to listen to Noah's good news and his warning about the hurricane/typhoon weather forecast that had been foretold by Noah for approximately 120 years! Allow me to point out some facts about the ark's construction:

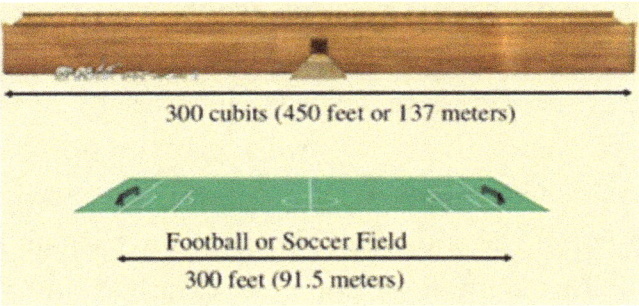

300 cubits (450 feet or 137 meters)

Football or Soccer Field
300 feet (91.5 meters)

The ark likely measured from 437 feet to 512 feet in length! God was the architect; therefore, it would be impossible for the ship to capsize.

The ark had three stories, with only one door to enter and exit. Scripture tells us that after construction, it was Father God who closed the door of the ark!

If Noah started building the ark soon after God spoke to him, then the construction may have taken close to 120 years.

Additionally, the spiritual meaning of the ark emphasizes:

The ark of Noah presents a type of salvation provided by Christ, who today is our ark of safety from God's future court sentencing of those who choose to reject the good news of salvation.

There was only one door to enter the ark, just as there is only one way to God, and that is through Christ Jesus. *I am the door of the sheep* (John 10:7). Jesus said that He is *the way, the truth, and the life* (John 14:6).

Based on observation, would you conclude that everyone who was in the ark was saved? The answer is quite obvious: of course! Therefore, all who were in the ark were protected from the massive waters of God's judgment. Secondly, we can conclude that the ark represents Christ, the Messiah, a place of safety and salvation for all who enter into Him by faith.

Noah's ark was the same vessel that saved both his family and the animals from God's judgment. Likewise, both man and animals (creation in general) are saved through the ark of Jesus Christ!

The animals are a component of the eternal family, and they will be an intrinsic part of His eternal "Global Family Government" of Jesus, our Messiah! I realize that these previous paragraphs are weighty thoughts for some to digest. However, if you read the account of Noah and the flood closely, it is quite clear that both man (Noah's family) and animals were saved in the ark!

We must understand that Father God has created animals for a purpose and according to His plan, both for this life and for the eternal life to come. Wait...you still don't think there are animals in heaven?

It is crystal clear that the believer's resurrection and the redemption of our bodies will bring deliverance not only to us, but also to the entirety of God's creation. Creation itself is groaning and travailing in suffering in anticipation of the transformation of the sons of Man, the redemption of men and women of faith in Christ!

*(Romans 8:19–23, CJB) The creation waits eagerly for the sons of God to be revealed; [20] for the creation was made subject to frustration – not willingly, but because of the one who subjected it. But it was given a reliable hope [21] **that it too would be set free from its bondage to decay** and would enjoy the freedom accompanying the glory that God's children will have. [22] We know that until now, the whole creation has been groaning as with the pains of childbirth; [23] and not only it, but we ourselves, who have the first fruits of the Spirit, groan inwardly as we continue waiting eagerly to be made*

sons – that is, to have our whole bodies redeemed and set free.

These passages seem to indicate that, through the newly God-reengineered Earth system, after and simultaneously with the resurrection of the men and women of faith, animals, who were subjected to the "old, cursed Earth system," will undergo a spectacular metamorphosis, a transformation amid the bodily resurrection of believers in Christ! Thereby, they will participate in the glorious freedom from the power of death and obliteration! You might say that the proverbial stranglehold on all creation is supernaturally eradicated – no more death – with the liberation that comes from the complete fulfillment of the resurrected Christians into a permanent, immortal state!

As I asked in the preface to this book, if there were no animals in heaven, why does Jesus tell us in Revelation 19:14 that we (the people of faith) will return with the Messiah, *riding on white horses*? Where did these horses come from? It's much more of an act of faith to accept that Jesus will return to Earth on a white horse rather than a Jeep Wrangler Sahara! What do you think?

God created pets to be our companions. He gave them the ability to forgive and forget (from our understanding of forgiveness) so that even when we mistreat them, they are ready and willing to move on with a relationship with us once again.

Additional animals were created to provide their strength and abilities to serve us in various capacities. For centuries, animal strength was the primary source of power used in industry, agriculture, transportation, and for sustaining inherent family financial wealth.

Pets can be therapeutic and bring emotional healing from painful events in one's life.

Caring for an animal helps teach anyone, at any age, the responsibilities of protection and provision. Petting an animal can help calm those who are troubled in spirit and emotionally distressed. You might say that pets provide a form

53

of therapy for anger management and emotional support, with longer life expectancy!

God's word tells us that animal lives should be respected and not be the recipient of man's ill treatment. When we mishandle animals, we are mistreating the living creation that God has bestowed upon us and the awesome gift of life. When we mistreat animals, we acknowledge or display that we're not as clean on the inside. Proverbs 12:10 says, *A righteous man has regard [respect] for the life [well-being] of his animal, but a cruel person doesn't ...*

God desires us to be good stewards of all His creation. And Jesus indicated that *not a single sparrow falls to the ground without God's concern* (Matthew 10:29). Animals, along with mankind, were also instructed by Father God in Exodus 20:10 **to be granted rest on the Sabbath**. In general, as we follow the Man from Galilee, we are to *live honestly and to love mercy and to walk humbly with our creator* (Micah 6:8).

Do Pets Go to Heaven?

We have all lost a dear pet, whether it's a dog, a cat, a bird, or even a loyal horse. These pets become an integral part of our family structure, forming a special emotional and physical bond within the family unit. When our pet passes on, the personality of that pet lives on in our memory. Please note, however, that animals are not redeemed as are men and women who possess faith in Jesus!

Therefore, they are not in a glorified state as humans are when we take our last breath. According to the Bible, there is a "divine order to the resurrection events": Christ first, then the Christians, and then all creation. This is a study that we will not embark on in this book. However, there is **a divine order to the Resurrection of all God's creation!**

God's Word reveals that humans and animals are different by God's creative design. However, if we study Genesis, we discover that God brought the animals to Adam first as a source from which to seek a companion or relationship, *for it was not good for man to be alone!*

Let's check it out in the "Genesis Project." Why would the Lord even consider this as an option? Why not cause Adam to sleep right away and then remove his rib to create Eve, his wife? Why didn't God create both Adam and Eve at the same time? Questions to ponder...

Genesis 2:18–22 (NIV):
¹⁸The Lord God said, "It is not good for

the man to be alone. I will make a helper suitable for him."

[19]Now the Lord God had formed out of the ground all the wild animals and all the birds in the sky. He brought them to the man to see what he would name them; and whatever the man called each living creature, that was its name. [20]So the man gave names to all the livestock, the birds in the sky and all the wild animals. But for Adam no suitable helper was found. [21]So the Lord God caused the man to fall into a deep sleep; and while he was sleeping, he took one of the man's ribs and then closed up the place with flesh. [22]Then the Lord God made a woman from the rib he had taken out of the man, and he brought her to the man...

Do Animals Have Souls? The Breath of Life!

The main point of the Genesis text was to intensify that God considered animals as potential associates – a joint venture, one might say – with Adam's endeavors. However, none were suitable. Therefore, the overture still remains. Do animals have souls?

This question has been a subject of debate at some point in our lives, whether it be in church or a group Bible study. Many believe that animals do not have souls. However, I would like to encourage the reader with my biblical position that animals indeed have a precious "soul structure." Therefore, they exist in the hereafter. Permit me to begin our study with the Hebrew words *chay,* which means "living," and *nephesh,* which means the "soul," and the Greek word *psūchê,* which means "living soul."

We will demonstrate how *chay, nephesh,* and *psūchê* are used by reviewing these words in the original language from selected Scripture passages and in their context, thereby gaining a greater comprehension.

After we read the selected passage, we will follow up with a brief explanation about the passage. [I encourage the reader to conduct their own deeper research into the original Hebrew and Greek words concerning animals possessing a soul.]

Example 1 – Man as *nephesh*:

And the Lord God formed man of the dust of the ground, and breathed into his nostrils the breath of life; and man became a living [chay] *soul* [nephesh]. (Genesis 2:7)

Example 2 – Animals as *nephesh*:

Out of the ground the Lord God formed every beast of the field, and every fowl of the air; and *brought them unto Adam to see what he would call them: and whatsoever Adam called each **living** [chay] creature [soul or nephesh], that was the name thereof.* (Genesis 2:19)

Example 3 – Noah and *nephesh*:

*And with every **living creature** [nephesh] that is with you, of the fowl, of the cattle, and of every beast of the earth with you; from all that go out of the ark, to every beast of the earth.* (Genesis 9:10, also in 12, 15-16).

Animals have a "soul structure." The key words are **"living creature" [*nephesh*]**

Please note that the phrase "living creature" in Example 3 is identical to "living soul" in Genesis 2:7 (Example 1) and in the King James Bible, which is translated as **"living soul."**

Moreover, Genesis 2:7 indicates that ...the *Lord God breathed the breath of **life** [chay]; and man became a living **soul** [nephesh].* Once again, this reinforces the point that animals possess a God-given "soul structure."

It is also noteworthy to point out that the use of the different words demands a different translation from the Hebrew. For comparability, **life [chay]** is the physical existence, or bodily form, that interacts with its surrounding environment to keep the physical form working. In contrast, the life force, or **soul [nephesh]**, comprises personality

58

traits that make us wonderfully unique from one another, representing the inner essence of who we are as individuals. Therefore, *nephesh* is translated as "soul."

Example 4 – New Testament:

(1 Corinthians 15:45, KJV) *And so it is written, the first man Adam was made a* **living soul [psūchê];** *the last Adam was made a quickening spirit.*

(Matthew 16:26, KJV) Jesus asked His followers, *"For what is a man profited, if he shall gain the whole world, and lose his own* **soul [psūchê]***?"*

The Old Testament definition of **"soul" [nephesh]** is translated in the New Testament as **"psūchê,"** the Greek equivalent. It is therefore based on the definition established in the Old Testament.

Special note: The Hebrew word for **soul, "nephesh,"** refers to the element of our unseen spirit that **lives on** after our physical body breathes its last breath.

These aforementioned passages amplify and authenticate that animals have a "soul" structure [**psūchê**]. This would logically establish that Adam and Eve were responsible for the care and well-being of the animal kingdom and had dominion over them. *Why?* Because animals have a lesser "soul structure" in comparison to man's.

My point is that animals and selected created forms in heaven and on earth possess a **psūchê** [soul], having experienced the breath of life given to them as a God-created "soul structure" (Genesis 2:7). We will examine this line of thought ("soul structure") further.

Reflective Note About the Soul!

As believers, we should humbly recognize and be in total awe of our Creator, Father God. Why? For our finite minds fall short of fully comprehending and completely understanding how God masterfully, artistically, and with extraordinary feats of biotechnology and pneumatology, engineered and created a **bodily** form with a **soul** and a **spirit** within mankind and the animals!

Moreover, He somehow made these three divisions function and network synergistically, whereby we have life!

Furthermore, one day in the future, God will marvelously resurrect our mortal bodies and supernaturally re-engineer our body, soul, and spirit into perpetual immortality!

My purpose with this note is to encourage contemplation on God's wondrous, creative engineering capability. How did God make a soul? What is the component of a soul by which to reverse engineer it? Where is it located in the body? These questions would apply to both mankind and animals!

In addition, I do not have the absolute answer to how God, our creator, makes the body, soul, and spirit of his created beings operate. It is far greater than my finite mind can understand.

God Created "Soul Structure"

Animals and humans have the "breath of life" or, as we say in the 21st century, a "life force" in them, as clearly stated in (Genesis 2:7; 6:17; & 7:15, 22).

However, I must emphatically stress that this position does not equate animals with human beings. Only mankind possesses an internal moral compass or a God-given ethical conscience.

In the Bible, Father God makes it perfectly clear: *He created man in His image.* This (man's soul) is utterly different from the "lesser soul structure" of animals. (I am addressing the term *"soul structure"* to stress that animals have a soul [**psūchê**], **but not like man's).** Therefore, we must by no means equate animals with humans. To do so would imply that animals were made

61

in the image of God. This line of thought should be abandoned altogether and is absolutely not biblically supported at all.

Let me reiterate it once again. Animals do not have a soul like mankind. However, let me point out what Scripture says. Some of God's creations have been engineered with a "soul structure" (Note: "the fleshly body" is the house for our inner soul or life force [**nephesh**].

This concept is amplified in 1 Corinthians 15:39 (ASV). *All flesh is not the same flesh, but there is one flesh of men, and another flesh of beasts, and another flesh of birds, and another of fish.*

God's word tells us there are "flesh types" created by His artist's engineering design. They have been formed with their own classification when fashioned, and some have been engineered with a simple "soul structure" with their bodily form.

Why do I say "simple soul structure"? Only a soul can contain a personality. Tethered with it will be the solid, evidentiary expressions of happiness, loyalty, anger, pain, guilt, sadness, levels of grief, a sense of obedience and disobedience, and a desire to save another life or help another being. Plus, there will be a rationalization of cognitive problem-solving abilities in certain situations. If

62

these traits are present, it then seems logical to believe, based on the preceding biblical pages, that our pets possess a soul (a "soul structure")!

Once again, my central point with this Scripture reference was to clarify that **"the flesh" is just the house where the soul lives!** Only a soul-filled entity will display affections and manifold emotions! Whereas, a soulless creation will not display any evidence of a personality or emotional interactions!

We can observe and consider these straightforward facts in the comfort of our own homes while interacting with our faithful pets. It is truly self-evident what entity has a soul and what does not!

Before the Fall

Additionally, before the fall of man and the curse of sin entered into man with all creation, an animal's emotional personality and "soul structure" were in a much more advanced and unencumbered form than what we know today. Moreover, the animals were able to form peaceful relationships and communion with mankind.

Furthermore, the term "soul structure" is reminiscent of what Christendom has historically referred to as God the Father, God the Son, and

63

God the Holy Spirit – known as "The Trinity" – for centuries, even though the word "trinity" is not found in the Holy Scripture.

However, the concept and tangible facts are remarkably present throughout. The word "rapture" is also not present in Scripture, but the principle is incredibly present. I think you understand my point!

I believe the best way to explain my position that animals and other created entities have a soul/life force within them is by elucidating with the words "God created **soul structure**," thereby helping the reader understand the study point with clarity! This leads me into my next thought on that same line.

Special thought: Angels hold a lower position than man, as inferred by scriptural evidence. It is unmistakably designated that they possess a "soul structure" but not the same one as man! God's word explains that the promise of the resurrection takes place when believers in Christ are both positioned higher than the angels and physically stronger than the heavenly host. Why? Because all believers will have a new body precisely like the Lord Jesus Christ.

Philippians 3:21 (KJV), Who shall change our vile body, that it may be fashioned like unto His glorious body, according to the working whereby He is able even to subdue all things unto Himself.

Therefore, the believer, in his/her resurrection body, is higher than angels. (also see Ephesians 1:3-23, and 1 Corinthians 15:39-57)

My point with this line of thought was to briefly amplify that angels and other created beings mentioned in God's word, such as the four living creatures (Revelation 4:6-9, 5:6-14, 6:1-8, 14:3, 15:7, and 19:4) have a "soul structure"! It is greater than that of the animals but lesser than that of the believer in Christ.

Angels have emotions, with divine characteristics that are very similar to those of humans. Based on what is currently revealed to us about them in God's word, they seem to follow specific instructions from the heavenly, fourth-dimensional realm, and only reveal their intentions in our third-dimensional realm when ordered to do so. (Daniel 10:11-13, and the Book of Revelation)

However, Scripture neither confirms nor denies that they are made in the image of God. This is a separate biblical study, which we will not focus on in this book. This would be another fascinating and interesting study to investigate!

Finally, I hope that explaining the term "soul structure," as defined by the words *nephesh* and *psūchê*, will highlight the fact that certain created entities possess soul-like qualities, as previously mentioned.

When God brought the animals to Adam, *there was no suitable helper for man.*

In other words, Adam was unable to establish a "million-dollar match." One of the interpretations of this "let's find a co-worker scene" in Scripture was to illustrate that each animal category type would be presented to Adam with its helpmate (counterpart) of the same nature, appearance, and characteristics.

Adam himself was missing his suitable counterpart, as he noticed when Father God brought animal friends to Adam's home.

But for Adam there was not found an help meet for him. (Genesis 2:20, KJV)

The word "meet" means, in modern terms, an equal, a companion, a sharer of his beliefs, feelings, observations, joys, purposes, and enterprises, as well as for procreation. It was evident, based upon his survey of the animals, that none of them was appropriate. They might be ministers to his industrial endeavors; however, there was no suitable helpmate compatible with Adam. In addition to giving names to the animals, Adam was establishing harmony and a family-structured relationship with the animal kingdom.

My central point in introducing these Genesis passages is to establish that Father God was displaying the principal importance of presenting the family of created animals to Adam.

Remember, my friends: At the time of creation, animals were not a part of man's dietary regimen. It consisted of only fruits and vegetables, all organically grown, I might add.

*Genesis 2: ^{9}The LORD God made all kinds of trees grow out of the ground – trees that were pleasing to the eye **and good for food**...^{15}The LORD God took the man and put him in the Garden of Eden to work it and take care of it. ^{16}And the LORD God commanded the man, **You are free to eat from any tree in the garden** [not animals].*

Furthermore, in the beginning, the animals were not intended to be mankind's sustainable food source but part of a cooperative family partnership with mankind, existing in perfect peace and accord!

The kingdom of God was with man at this time, before sin's weapons of mass destruction and chaos appeared.

Only after the fall of man were animals a food source, and they would also be instituted as part of the Israelites' gifts and sacrificial traditions.

This foreshadowed Christ's ultimate and final sacrifice for mankind's sin. (Kindly reference the Book of Hebrews chapters 5:1-5 & chapters 8,9,10 for a summary explanation of the Old Testament subject of gifts and animal sacrifices before Christ's ultimate and final sacrifice.)

Scripture indicates that animals were mostly innocent at the time of the fall. Why do I write "mostly"? The Scripture tells us that only Adam and Eve hid from the Lord after they disobeyed.

There is no mention of the animals hiding except for one. In Genesis 3:8-11, the serpent was used by Satan to tempt Eve. The serpent was held accountable for allowing the Devil to use its form in the temptation act with Eve. Furthermore, that animal was cursed with a noted physical change to his bodily form when God pronounced his judgment on all involved in the sinful act.

Genesis 3:1-4, Then the LORD God said to the serpent: Because you have done this, you are cursed more than any livestock and more than any animal. You will move on your belly and eat dust all the days of your life.

Please note: Before the serpent was cursed, it seems logical to surmise that it did not crawl on its belly or in the dust. Perhaps it was able to consistently fly or walk to the tree of knowledge to talk with Eve. Why do I say "consistently"? Because Eve was not surprised that the serpent was communicating, and both were present in the exact geographical location. (This concept is a separate biblical study that we will not focus on in this book, though it is an interesting subject to explore!)

My point in sharing this was to convey that one animal received a special form of judgment.

Nevertheless, creation and the animal kingdom received the collateral damage of Adam's and Eve's disobedience. They were ultimately cursed, currently infected with "the micro and macro curse, meaning entropy and the Second Law of Thermodynamics." This would be a separate Bible study, which we will not research in this book.

There is a fascinating story in Numbers 22:9-39 (ESV). Balaam was a seer; however, he was a corrupt prophet driven by love for money rather than being loyal to God. He had a reputation for cursing the opposing army, and it would come to pass that they would lose the battle.

Balak [King of Moab], an enemy of the Israelites, wanted to hire and compensate Balaam to curse Israel and conquer their land and people. However, the primary purpose in this story, for our investigation, is to focus on Balaam and his pet donkey.

<u>Balaam's Donkey and the Angel</u>

Balak sent officers, in number, and they came to Balaam and said to him, "Thus says Balak the son of Zippor: 'Let nothing hinder you from coming to me, for I will surely do you great honor, and whatever you say to me I will do. Come, curse this Israel people for me.'"

But Balaam answered and said to the servants of Balak, "Though Balak were to give me his house full of silver and gold, I could not go beyond the command of the Lord my God to do less or more. So, you, too, please stay here tonight, that I may know what the Lord will say to me." And God came to Balaam at night and said to him, "If the men that have come ask you to go with them, rise, go with them; but only do what I tell you."

So Balaam rose in the morning and saddled his donkey and went with the officers of Moab.

But God's anger was kindled because he went, and the angel of the Lord took his stand in the way as his adversary.

Now he was riding on the donkey, and his two servants were with him. And the donkey saw the angel of the Lord standing in the road, with a drawn sword in his hand. And the donkey turned aside away from the road and went into the field. And Balaam struck the donkey, to turn her back into the road.

71

Then the angel of the Lord stood in a narrow path between the vineyards, with a wall on either side. And when the donkey saw the angel of the Lord, she pushed against the wall and pressed Balaam's foot against the wall. So he struck her again.

Then the angel of the Lord went ahead and stood in a narrow place, where there was no way to turn either to the right or to the left. When the donkey saw the angel of the Lord, she lay down under Balaam. And Balaam's anger was kindled, and he struck the donkey with his staff.

*Then the Lord opened the mouth of the donkey, and she said to Balaam, "**What have I done to you, that you have struck me these three times**?" And Balaam said to the donkey, "Because you have made a fool of me. I wish I had a sword in my hand, for then I would kill you." And the donkey said to Balaam, "Am I not your donkey, on which you have ridden all your life long to this day? Is it my habit to treat you this way?" And he said, "No."*

Then the Lord opened the eyes of Balaam, and he saw the angel of the Lord standing in the way, with his drawn sword in his hand. And he bowed down and fell on his face. And the angel of the Lord said to him, "Why have you struck your donkey these three times? Behold, I have come out to oppose you because your way is perverse before me.

The donkey saw me and turned aside before me these three times. If she had not turned aside from me, surely just now I would have killed you and let her live."

Then Balaam said to the angel of the Lord, "I have sinned, for I did not know that you stood in the road against me. Now therefore, if it is evil in your sight, I will turn back." And the angel of the Lord said to Balaam, "Go with the men, but speak only the word that I tell you." So Balaam went on with the princes of Moab.

Didn't I tell you this is an interesting story? It seems that God reveals the thoughts and intentions of the donkey to a rogue prophet. Balaam was a prophet who aligned himself with a colleague by the name of Balak, who insisted that Balaam come to see him and curse [wish bad fortune on] the children of Israel.

However, God didn't approve it. Subsequently, as Balaam rode his donkey along the dirt road to visit his friend Balak, the angel of the Lord

73

stood right in his path, effectively blocking his way, holding in his hand a double-edged sword positioned for execution! Balaam, the prophet of God, couldn't see the angelic host; however, the donkey was cognizant of the angel of the Lord and three times turned off the dirt path to avoid a confrontation. When the donkey changed course, Balaam was angry and beat his pet for this erratic behavior.

This is the part that gets very interesting. The Lord miraculously opened the mouth of the donkey, and she said to Balaam the prophet, *"What have I done to you, that you have struck me these three times?"*

In a nutshell, the donkey was moving out of the way of the angel of the Lord to save the life of the prophet. However, the Lord opened the vocal cords of the animal, enabling her to vocalize and articulate in human language, giving us insight into her thoughts and reasoning. She confronts Balaam the prophet as to why he was beating her without just cause.

This Scripture is truly awe-inspiring. Why do I say this? I believe it is a revelation as to what awaits us in the heavenly kingdom of Jesus Christ! **The fact that animals are able to communicate in human language is a totally exciting biblical concept!** I amplify this concept predicated on the fact that the Lord gave the donkey the ability to speak as a human being, and the donkey said what she was feeling at that point in time. **Therefore, this is further evidence that pets have a soul! Only a soul-filled entity can communicate its thoughts and emotions. Would you not agree?** We all know that animals converse among their own kind in their own unique languages.

Therefore, the Lord gave the donkey the capacity to speak her mind. In my opinion, the donkey may have already had these offended thoughts and feelings in (not to be comical) "donkey language," but she was unable to speak them in human language at the time of her beatings!

I would like to add this thought. When we receive our glorious bodies, **we will possess new and exciting abilities, including the comprehension of all forms of languages,** meaning we could talk to the animals, too! Remember, we will possess every eternal characteristic of Jesus; however, we will not have His creative authority to engineer a life or soul-filled being.

Now, this was not a "super donkey." It was simply an animal whose spirit could observe into the fourth-dimensional realm. Moreover, with the Lord's permission, she was able to speak human language.

75

I would like to share one more heart-warming dog story. I believe it would be fitting to introduce another example of how our pets possess a soul structure.

Our story begins in Japan in the early 1900s with a college professor named Mr. Ueno. After his daily morning routine of walking and playing with his Akita, Hachikō, he would leave for work via the local train. Hachikō would stand by the bamboo front door to watch him go off to work while keeping Mrs. Ueno company during the day.

By the end of the workday, Mr. Ueno looked forward to meeting his favorite pet as he arrived at the train station in his hometown, usually about four o'clock.

Back at home, Hachikō knew it was nearing four o'clock and his master would be arriving at the train station. He was filled with excitement and would leap over the brown, one-foot-high backyard fence and fly like a rocket to the train station to warmly greet his master! Then they would walk back home together.

From the passing of winter to spring, from summer to the painted color pattern of the falling leaves, the pages of their lives would turn as Hachikō joyfully greeted his master at the old train station day after day. Mr. Ueno would treasure these memorable arrivals, for each one would bring great joy while walking home.

Then on a late, hazy, cloudy afternoon in May, Mr. Ueno, while teaching at the university, frantically gripped his forehead with his hands and fell to the brown oak floor.

Several students ran out of class to the nurses' room on campus. Nurse Kyoko immediately dialed the paramedics. When they arrived, they tried to save Mr. Ueno; however, they were too late, and he died. It was later discovered that he had given up his spirit from a massive stroke.

Later in the afternoon, Hachikō leaped over the backyard fence with the same excitement as in times past and ran to greet his beloved master coming home from work. As always, Hachikō sat with a pleasing smile and prepared his furry paws to greet his owner as he stepped off the train car. However, the hours slowly passed without Hachikō seeing his beloved master exit through the train car doors. He continued patiently waiting for many more hours for his master to walk off the train.

Eventually, a family member realized that someone must go to Hachikō and carry him back home. The Akita didn't understand that his kind master had departed this life for the big train station in the sky.

The Long Wait

Now the next day brought a sunny, beautifully filled blue sky, marking the beginning of an act of dedication where this loyal dog would return to the small, local train station every day, month after month, year after long year, unwearied and still awaiting his master's return.

History tells us that Hachikō became such a familiar presence at the town's train station that the stationmaster set out food for the dog and gave him a bed there.

Even so, Hachikō, by no means, shifted loyalties. Every day at four o'clock, he waited hopefully by the tracks as the train pulled in. His little brown eyes searched for his master's face among the crowd of people getting off the train.

After nine long years of waiting faithfully for his master at the railway station, Hachikō was now old and weakened. Still, he continued to go to the railway station, where he waited devotedly day after day, without fail, hoping to see his master step off the train and greet him once again. Hachikō eventually died after ten faithful years. Nevertheless, the dog's steadfast spirit of family loyalty would not be forgotten. A year before his death, Shibuya (Shi-bu-ya) Train Station staff and local town officials installed a bronze statue of the aging dog to honor the station's mascot and to serve as a reminder of the loyalty of our beloved family pets!

Final Thoughts

I am applying this story to amplify and tether all the aforementioned data in this chapter and the previous together to show that animals possess a *nephesh* – they are a "living being." They have a soul.

There is no doubt that such a relationship between a pet and its owner is truly astonishing! However, that's not the end of it. How could an animal have the fortitude and diligence for ten years straight, like clockwork, to maintain the same faithfulness, loyalty, and devotion if they did not have a soul? And while the owner was not alive!

Dogs, cats, horses, elephants, dolphins, and other animals have differing degrees of emotion and personality characteristics, which is evident that they possess a soul!

When our pet displays their exuberant, joyful greeting, it is to welcome a formerly missing family member! Our return is celebrated, even though we may have gone to the supermarket or to work for only a couple of hours.

Their excitement is awe-inspiring and brings forth joyfulness in our spirit, too, when we are greeted with such elated exuberance! Again, this strengthens the point that they have a *nephesh*, or a soul!

With the finest spirited emotions, our pets are capable of deciphering thoughts and deep feelings. In other words, they have cognitive problem-solving capabilities with the capacity to intellectually comprehend their owner's pain, worries, fears, grief, etc. With these abilities, they can give us, their owners, comfort and solace during difficult times in our lives.

I am sure you can recollect personally or from another's account similar acts of pet faithfulness, protection, and loyalty!

The foregoing narrative reveals and amplifies God's word on this subject matter, which is that animals have a *nephesh* – "living creature" – or possess a "soul structure," as discussed early in this chapter.

This statement is predicated on the facts and outflow of emotional interactions such as joy, sadness, loyalty, devotion, protection, and faithfulness. Once again, my friends, all attributes of possessing a soul structure! Again, I point out, not like the soul of mankind, who are made in God's image, as previously noted in this chapter.

This brings us to our next exciting idea: the joyful expectation that our pets' emotional and personality depth will be extraordinarily enriched! Why do I write this? They, too, will be a particular part of the eternal kingdom of our creator, Father God! Please read Isaiah 11:6-9 and 65:25 for additional information about animals in God's word.

CHAPTER 4

THE RESURRECTION

Animals will most definitely be in attendance during the millennial kingdom (Rev. 21:1). God promises a resurrection homecoming to their original creative state, similar to before the fall with the entrance of sin, in a never-ending, immortal condition. Father God declares to us in Luke 20:38, *"He is not a God of the dead, but of the living."*

The absolute essence of the Father is summarized in four simple words: "The Creator of Life." John tells us in his Gospel that Jesus is the bread of life, the living water, the resurrection, and the life. We read in 1 John 5:12, "He that hath the Son hath life."

"Life" is what the Father, the Son, and the Holy Spirit are all about, my friends! Living is of paramount importance to Father God. Marvelously, in the word of God, we can discover a full understanding of what happens to all of God's creation at the resurrection. Let us read what Father God tells us in 1 Corinthians 15:35-58 (NIV)

> *But someone will ask, "How are the dead raised? With what kind of body will they come?" How foolish! What you sow does not come to life unless it dies. When you sow, you do not plant the body that will be, but just a seed, perhaps of wheat or of something else. But God gives it a body as he has determined, and to each kind of seed he gives its own body. Not all flesh is the same: People have one kind of*

flesh, animals have another, birds another and fish another. There are also heavenly bodies and there are earthly bodies; but the splendor of the heavenly bodies is one kind, and the splendor of the earthly bodies is another. The sun has one kind of splendor, the moon another and the stars another; and star differs from star in splendor.

So will it be with the resurrection of the dead. The body that is sown is perishable, it is raised imperishable; it is sown in dishonor, it is raised in glory; it is sown in weakness, it is raised in power; it is sown a natural body, it is raised a spiritual body.

If there is a natural body, there is also a spiritual body. So it is written: "The first man Adam became a living being"; the last Adam, a life-giving spirit. The spiritual did not come first, but the natural, and after that the spiritual. The first man was of the dust of the earth; the second man is of heaven. As was the earthly man, so are those who are of the earth; and as is the heavenly man, so also are those who are of heaven. And just as we have borne the image of the earthly man, so shall we bear the image of the heavenly man.

I declare to you, brothers, and sisters,

that flesh and blood cannot inherit the kingdom of God, nor does the perishable inherit the imperishable. Listen, I tell you a mystery: We will not all sleep, but we will all be changed—in a flash, in the twinkling of an eye, at the last trumpet. For the trumpet will sound, the dead will be raised imperishable, and we will be changed. For the perishable must clothe itself with the imperishable, and the mortal with immortality. When the perishable has been clothed with the imperishable, and the mortal with immortality, then the saying that is written will come true: "Death has been swallowed up in victory."

"Where, O death, is your victory? Where, O death, is your sting?" The sting of death is sin, and the power of sin is the law. But thanks be to God!

He gives us the victory through our Lord Jesus Christ. Therefore, my dear brothers and sisters, stand firm. Let nothing move you. Always give yourselves fully to the work of the Lord, because you know that your labor in the Lord is not in vain.

The Quintessence

Our physical body, the bodies of animals, and celestial bodies' quantum particles are all extremely important to Father God. He reveals to us that He cares about *all of His creation!* It seems that God's engineering design will eternally be with us in a brilliantly miraculous and absolutely glorified state of being, transforming this currently broken and messed-up universal system.

God will not forsake the body. He will raise our bodies as believers; therefore, *the groaning of all His creation will cease.* Why? Creation will have similar resurrection benefits, as men and women of faith in Christ *the Messiah will have!* - Romans 8:19-24 as reference)

Wow! What an extraordinary and amazing calendar day that will be! The Master and Creator re-engineering His ultimate family-planning initiative!

In this chapter, I will support the belief that animals will be part of the resurrection by educating the reader on the following verses. These passages give factual support for the resurrection, presupposing that all creative life will be included. However, the emphasis is on men and women of faith in Messiah Christ! Let us begin with 1st Corinthians 15:35-44

But someone will ask, "How are the dead raised? With what kind of body will they come?" How foolish! What you sow does not come to life unless it dies. When you sow, you do not plant the body that will be, but just a seed, perhaps of wheat or of something else. But God gives it a body as he has determined, and to each kind of seed he gives its own body. Not all flesh is the same: People have one kind of flesh, animals have another, birds another and fish another. There are also heavenly bodies and there are earthly bodies; but the splendor of the heavenly bodies is one kind, and the splendor of the earthly bodies is another. The sun has one kind of splendor, the moon another and the stars another; and star differs from star in splendor.

So, will it be with the resurrection of the dead. The body that is sown is perishable, it is raised imperishable; it is sown in dishonor, it is raised in glory; it is sown in weakness, it is raised in power; it is sown a natural body, it is raised a spiritual body.

<u>A Kernel</u>

Now we'll park here for a moment. The depiction of a seed in these scriptures provides a great picture for us to imagine. Whenever a seed is planted in the ground and watered, it brings forth life. Father God exemplifies the resurrection concept with the theory of harvest. By this example, picture a farmer sowing (planting) a seed.

First, however, the seed must "die." Then it lives (or is resurrected) when it is planted in the ground. The seed, combined with soil, sun, and water, will then be transformed into something entirely new!

In other words, whatever seed you sow, you are going to get that kind of life from that seed. Furthermore, the plant that is produced will be very different in appearance from the tiny seed when it was initially planted in the soil.

As we continue this line of thought, check out what 1 Corinthians 15:38 (NIV) says, *"But God gives it a body as he has determined, and to each kind of seed he gives its own body."*

This is an awesome example. Why do I write this? Well, the complete matter of resurrection is predicated on the exclusive power of Father God, and the resurrection process is solely in the Father's hands. God can furnish any person, animal, or celestial entity with what He wants to provide it with, correct? That is a fundamental truth that we're exploring here concerning the resurrection. God can do anything He wants when it comes to resurrection!

Think about it—God can take one little humble

seedling and marvelously transform it, as is evident when it breaks through the earth's crust. When a resurgence takes place, that seedling appears completely different from the way it looked when it was planted in the ground and covered in the soil of the earth.

This resurrection of all life is orchestrated by God's prerogative, predicated on our faith; implementing this resurrection gives our Father immense pleasure and gladness! My friends, the purposefully engineered "resurrection of life" is what our heavenly Father desires to fully perform! Life is what Father God is all about!

By the way, He says that every *seed has its own body*. Father God is telling us that every person and animal has its own personal body type. Remember, all human hands possess a God-created genetic fingerprint, wonderfully different and distinct from each other and from the billions of people on Earth.

Likewise, this resurrection applies to the animal kingdom. They, too, possess specific, distinctive personal identification characteristics that demonstrate each animal's unique individuality. For example, take the Bengal tiger and a zebra. Both have stripes, but both are different animals. Alternatively, consider the horse and the donkey; they are similar, yet the donkey has longer ears, a distinct tail, and other features that set it apart from the horse.

You know something interesting about this verse, *"to each kind of seed he gives its own body"*? We cannot fully comprehend what our resurrected body will look like, meaning, you will still be *you*, but a new and improved version of you, both inside and out!

The Father's basic point here is that He can bestow a new body as He desires at the time of the resurrection of the dead! When we meditate further on God's seed illustration, we observe that when the seedling is planted and breaks through the earth's crust, after reaching full maturity, they are beautifully, incredibly, and utterly different in bodily form than when the seed was planted into the soil.

Likewise, when we (Christians) with all God's creation are resurrected, it will be like having an extraordinary gift on Christmas Day waiting to be opened! All creation will receive the greatest of all Christmas gifts—**never-ending life and health!**

Can you envision what it will be like when we receive our brand-spanking-new, never-to-grow-old, and never-again-sickened-with-illness bodies! That is why Father God employs the seed illustration. We are unable to comprehend intellectually and completely what our new body, with all living creation, will appear like on the resurrection/transformation day!

Yes, the seed is truly a fantastic picture. That tiny seed is humble when it enters the earth's soil. Then, when it breaks through the surface and fully matures, it is raised in a different kind of spectacular glory!

Let us move on to the next line of thought and look at the form of "the resurrection." We can understand further about resurrection in verses 39–41:

> Not all flesh is the same: People have one kind of flesh, animals have another, birds another and fish another. There are also heavenly bodies and there are earthly bodies; but the splendor of the heavenly bodies is one kind, and the splendor of the earthly bodies is another. The sun has one kind of splendor, the moon another and the stars another; and star differs from star in splendor."

These verses are interesting from the resurrection viewpoint! Father God is saying to us that there are various types of life forms, not all the same. When Father God finished creating all forms of life, they were *blessed*, and He called *good* what He saw (Gen. 1:31). When it comes to the construction business, God is a master creative engineer.

Now, let's look further into 1 Corinthians 15:39-41. He simply says, *"There's one kind of flesh of men, another flesh of beasts, another of fish, and another of birds."*

Verse 40 further expands this principle. Not only are there terrestrial bodies, such as animals and plants, but there are also celestial bodies, including heavenly bodies like the sun, the moon, and the stars.

> *"So will it be with the resurrection of the dead. The body that is sown perishable, it is raised imperishable; it is sown in fragility, it is raised in glory; it is sown in weakness, it is raised in power; it is sown a natural body, it is raised a spiritual body" (1 Corinthians 15:42-44).*

94

If you observe the pine tree seed chart, you will notice the humble seed, but when it comes alive, the leaves are completely different, determined by the type of seed. In verse 42, the Word says, *"So also is the resurrection of the dead."*

Father God is sharing with us that there is a huge difference, yes, a huge difference between this old body and our new resurrected one!

Totally exciting! —The resurrection bodies of men and women who choose Jesus as their Savior and Lord, the animal kingdom, and the celestial kingdom are going to be enormously and vastly different from what you see, hear, taste, smell, and feel in this current earthly mortal existence, guaranteed!

Why do I write this? Well, the glory of the resurrection body will most definitely and very infinitely go beyond anything we can conceive or imagine! That would include the animal kingdom, too!

Let me say it this way. When you see your new resurrected, radiant body shining like the stars in heaven, it will be vastly different from your current earthly suit, which is like a humble seed!

Remember, the inner spirit (your soul) is housed within your current physical body; therefore, the real redeemed you is amalgamated with God the Holy Spirit. When Jesus entered your heart by faith, God the Holy Spirit resides within your soul.

Why do I write this? Because Ephesians 5:32 tells us of a *"great mystery"* between Christ and the church. What does that mean? This profound mystery is the amalgamation of you and Jesus becoming one!

Let me explain it this way: the seed of the Word of God, combined with the conscious action of your heart with faith in Christ, brings forth the conception of the new birth! This occurs in conjunction with and simultaneously to the Holy Spirit taking up residency and becoming intrinsically amalgamated in your heart and soul. Therefore, as Christ was resurrected from the dead, so likewise you too will be raised from this mortality to immortality in Christ!

The Holy Spirit within you is a deposit (an engagement ring, a down payment of sorts) of all the promises from Father God. He stipulates from His word that He will fully provide for you, both in this life and in the resurrected life to come, guaranteed! (Kindly Read Ephesians 1:13-14.)

Currently, we reside in and work from a corruptible "clay house." However, at the resurrection of our bodies, we will be given a unique, novel, and glorified biological body, far different from what we've ever seen before in this earthly life.

Let us not limit Father God with human comprehension, for He possesses limitless biotech genetic engineering capabilities and the quantum mechanics of creating life!

Just as numerous seeds vary, so likewise, our earthly bodies vary. Therefore, our resurrection bodies will have an immortal glory all their own! God is not restricted. If He promises it, He absolutely can accomplish it. Guaranteed!

When our perishable earthly bodies have been transformed into heavenly bodies that will never die, then at last the Scriptures will come true:

"Death is swallowed up in victory. O death, where is your victory? O death, where is your sting?"
—*1 Corinthians 15:54–55*

These are exciting verses to read and digest, truly food for the soul! "So, when this corruptible shall have put on incorruption, and this mortal has put on immortality, then shall be brought to pass the saying that is written: Death is swallowed up in victory"

Paul says, *"There is coming a resurrection transformation day for all of God's creation! We are going to be radically transformed via a spiritual metamorphosis (the* author's paraphrase).

97

Father God promises that this absolutely fantastic event unequivocally is going to happen! **There will be a day with no more decay, no more dying. All of the Father's creation will become a never-ending, everlasting, eternal state of being!**

Revelation 21:1-7 tells us that when this happens, death shall be no more. There will be no more sorrow, no more pain, no more sickness, and no more death. Father God will take this corruptible creation, this mortal state, overturn and reverse it, making you and me something that we have never seen before (author's paraphrase).

This is only possible because we are in Christ, and since we are His, we shall become incorruptible! Immortality shall be granted to all who are written in the Lamb's Book of Life! What that tells me is that our resurrection is a future event similar to our own personal Fourth of July fireworks! Alternatively, imagine your most exciting, thrilling, awe-inspiring feeling in the depths of your life, and multiply that one million-fold.

You may be wondering what our bodies will be like when glorified. Additionally, what will the animal bodies look like? Regarding men and women who place their complete trust and faith in Jesus Christ, the Messiah, we will have a body like the body of Jesus Christ when He came out of the grave.

What an incredible reflection! When you die as a believer, your spirit goes to be with Christ; however, you await the day when Christ comes to take you by the hand and pull you out of that dirty, rotten, filthy graveyard, and give you a brand spanking new glorified body, reunited with your redeemed and glorified soul! Whereby, we will always be with Christ and His administration, the CEO of the universe, in perpetual peace!

Totally awesome! Jesus Christ not only conquered death, but He also made a way for us and His creations to conquer it through Him, as God tells us, *"This corruptible will become incorruptible."*

Can you imagine no more dying, no more sickness, and no more pain? Someday, the *sting and the power of death will be totally removed,* and death will be completely kaput. All of those who are Christ's will be liberated from death and receive glorified bodies. We wait in glorious anticipation of the concrete fact that the *sting of death is removed and the grave is unlocked.* What a huge victory for all created life!

In our current state of being, we all realize

that death still has a sting, doesn't it? You had somebody die in your family, and it stings our souls. Death still hurts. We hate to imagine dying or witnessing someone gasping their last breath. However, be of good courage; someday the grip of death will end. In the future, death will breathe its last breath. That will be the glorious hour when death is folded up like a blanket and burned up to smithereens.

Another theological note: death was finished when Jesus rose from the dead. Why do I write this? Paul teaches us in Romans 6:9, *"Knowing that Christ being raised from the dead...he dieth no more."*

Why? Because the power of death has no more dominion over Him or those who have faith in Messiah Jesus! How? Jesus has the keys to death's door! Moreover, there will be absolutely no more fatalities. Paul tells us that death will be the final enemy to be destroyed.

Regarding the resurrection of the animal kingdom, we addressed this question earlier in the booklet. Will our much-loved pets be in heaven?

Let's look at what the prophet Isaiah wrote.

And the wolf shall dwell with the lamb, and the leopard shall lie down with the kid, and the calf and the young lion and the fatted domestic animal together; and a little child shall lead them. And the cow and the bear shall feed side by side, their young shall lie down together, and the lion shall eat straw like the ox. And the sucking child shall play over the hole of the asp, and the weaned child shall put his hand on the adder's den. They shall not hurt or destroy in all My holy mountain, for the earth shall be full of the knowledge of the Lord as the waters cover the sea. Isaiah 11:6-9, amp

Based on the fifteenth chapter of 1 Corinthians and passages found in Isaiah (Isaiah 11:6; 65:25), it seems exceptionally plausible and extremely probable that our family pets, whom we have loved in this earthly life, will be in heaven. Moreover, understanding that God is extremely just and all His decrees fair, it is also likely that when we enter the Father's house, we will find ourselves completely overwhelmed with a warm greeting, saying, "Welcome to Your New Home" by our loved ones who had faith in Jesus Christ, angelic host and of course our furry friends from long ago!

Why do I say and believe this?

Number one: The Genesis account of Father God creatively engineering life with both the human and animal kingdoms. The fact being that

101

they (mankind and the animals) were created to live in harmony and possess an eternal state of peace and happiness. Father will commence what He originally started at the beginning of creation, as defined in the first couple of chapters in the Book of Genesis.

Number two: Here's a consideration. Let us presuppose that when our pets die, they go to heaven because a loving and merciful God has ordained it that way (biblical proof aforementioned and to follow). Our pets have no "salvation understanding" as we have. Why? Because they do not require it—they are innocent and have not fallen from grace. They were part of God's creation in an innocent state. When Adam sinned with Eve, they passed "sin" on to all people, according to Romans Chapters 1–3. It doesn't say sin passed to the animals. They are, however, part of God's creation that is under *"the curse"* (collateral damage) caused by Adam's sin.

First Corinthians 2:9 (KJV) states, *"But as it is written, Eye hath not seen, nor ear heard, neither have entered into the heart of man, the things which God has prepared for them that love him."*

This is a beautifully exciting assurance from Father God to us! Evidently, what God has promised to prepare for us is extremely wonderful.

It's an enormous, super-sized promise—a

rock-solid guarantee! Think about it—these encouraging words are far above and beyond our intellectual comprehension or imagination! Father God and His Son Jesus prepared a new, peaceful, and joyful habitation for all His family and creation!

*Do not let your heart be troubled; believe [trust] in God, believe [trust] also in Me. In my Father's house are dwelling places; if it were not so, I would have told you; for **I go to prepare a place for you**. If I go and prepare a place for you, I will come again and receive you to Myself, that **where I am, there you may be also*** - John 14:1-3

This offers such a beautiful image! The Father's house is a prepared home of affection, hope, and trust! Home is where the heart is! It is that calm, secure place where those who love us, and whom we care for, dwell. It is a place of safety and positive encouragement.

Home is a place where the remedy of a troubled heart is the comfort of trusting in Jesus. "Let not your hearts be troubled." Why? When your life is falling apart, when broken dreams have crumbled, when a heavy heart weighs you down, God tells us, "Be of good courage, and the Lord will strengthen your heart to get back up."

The God of all comfort, who is unmoving and fully in control of all life events, who concretely knows what He is doing, will completely be able to comfort and console all our worried feelings and soothe our souls.

He promises, *"I go to prepare a place for you in my Father's house"* [author paraphrase]. It will be far greater than you can ever imagine or consider with your human mind! My friends, simply believe and trust the Lord. He is getting everything ready and preparing for a never-ending, everlasting, spectacular celebratory festivity for all His dear children of faith, guaranteed! Trust Him!

Therefore, be encouraged, all who take pleasure in their pets! Look enthusiastically forward to reuniting with them in their glorified, resurrected, never-ending, and eternal life state, in the perpetual condition that Father God originally created in the Garden of Eden! Mankind and animals will live in peace and harmony with their merciful creator and God, forever and ever, amen! Guaranteed!

CHAPTER 5

GOTTA HAVE FAITH!

I hope you enjoyed our little study about our faithful pets! Before we conclude, I would like to encourage you to reflect on the person of Jesus of Nazareth. The good news is that God has revealed that He loves you and all His creation.

He demonstrates His personal kindness for us by sending His Son [who volunteered by choice] to pay for our sins through execution on the cross. Then, after three days and nights, He was resurrected from the dirty grave, providing forgiveness for all our dirty deeds and messed-up decisions! This good news requires a personal response from your heart.

It's my intention to present God's Plan of Salvation clearly and understandably. Understanding and believing who Jesus says He is will be the most important undertaking any of us will ever face! It's truly the most critical decision we will ever make in our entire lives!

God's Simple Plan of Salvation

My friend, I am about to ask you the most important question of your life. Your joy or your sorrow for all eternity depends upon your choice. The question is, are you saved? It is not a question of how good you are, nor if you are a church member, but are you saved? Meaning, are you sure you will go to heaven when it's your turn to pass from this life to the next?

God says that, to go to heaven, you must

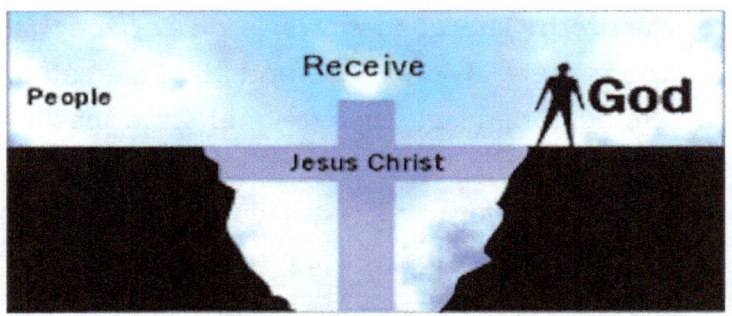

have a new birth. In John 3:7, Jesus said to Nicodemus [who was a religious leader, seeking answers on how to go to heaven], *"You must be born again."*

How can I be "born again"? In the Bible, God provides us with a plan for rebirth, which means being saved and prepared for heaven.

In other words, you had a natural birth via your mother and father when you physically entered this earthly realm. Likewise, you must be born again spiritually, by faith, to enter God's heavenly realm.

Salvation is predicated solely on the virtuous merits of Jesus Christ and on him only. His plan is simple! Marvelously, we can be saved anytime, anyplace, anywhere—even today. How?

First, my friend, we must realize we are all sinners. *"For all have sinned, and come short of the glory of God" (Romans 3:23).* Because we are sinners via our earthly nature, we are unable to save ourselves or go to heaven.

"For the wages [payment] of sin is death" (Romans 6:23). This includes eternal separation from God, in a dreadful place called hell. The Bible also says, *"It is appointed unto men once to die, but after we die God will judge our life* [emphasis added].... (Hebrews. 9:27).

"For what shall it profit a man, if he shall gain the whole world [house, car, power, fame], and lose his own soul? [emphasis added] (Mark 8:36). The commodity is our soul. The profit is determined by where you choose to invest it.

"He hath made him [Jesus, who knew no sin] to be sin for us [take the rap]] ...that we might be made the righteousness [right relationship with

God] of God in him" (2 Cor. 5:21), (Rom. 5:8). [emphasis added]

God said our sins were laid upon Jesus, and He died in our place. He became our substitute. My friend, *"God...encourages all men everywhere to have faith and believe"* (Acts 17:30, emphasis added).

This repentance is the changing of one's mind to agree with God that we lie, steal, and hurt others. However, the good news is that Father God loved you so much that He gave His only begotten Son, Jesus, to take the punishment for your wrongdoing and die in your place. Trusting in who Jesus says he is equals "faith and repentance." In Acts 16:30-31, the Philippians' jailer asked Paul and Silas, *"Sirs, what must I do to be saved? And they said, believe on the Lord Jesus Christ, and you will be saved.* – Also, in John 3:15-18 *-everyone who believes in him will* [definitely] have *eternal life.* (emphasis added). *"For this is how God loved the world that He gave his one and only Son, so that everyone who believes in him will not perish but have eternal life. God sent his Son into the world not to judge the world, but to save the world through him. "There is no judgment against anyone who believes in him. But anyone who does not believe in him has already been judged for not believing in God's one and only Son...*

108

<u>Receive Jesus Christ as Savior.</u>

If we understand and believe what we just read, then we are ready. If we take ownership of this information, then we can make a cognizant, mindful decision.

Please note that the steps below serve as a guide, pointing you to Jesus. Our salvation comes only through faith in Jesus, my friend! He alone has the power to save!

(#1) Recognize that we do wrong, deserving an eternal consequence for the same.

(#2) Desire to turn from our sin and be made clean

(#3) Understand that we are unable to make ourselves clean

(#4) Recognize the sacrifice of Jesus as our only means of forgiveness of wrongdoings and receiving the gift of eternal life!

(#5) Open the door of our heart and ask Him inside.

"Behold, I stand at the door and knock – if any one hears My voice and opens the door, I will come in to him." (Revelation 3:20, NKJV)

As many as received Him, to them He gave the right to become children of God, even to those who believe in His name. (John 1:12)

If you truly understand and believe, I urge you to ask Jesus into your life; let's not reschedule another date! *Today, if you hear His voice, do not have unbelief in your hearts. (Hebrews 3:15).*

Share with Him that you believe His sacrifice was the complete act of payment and forgiveness for your wrongdoings and ask Him to be your Savior. You have come this far in life; do not let another day go by without asking for the free gift of everlasting life!

There's no special prayer required. Simply tell Him from your heart that you believe, and ask Him to save you! Pray something like this:

Dear God, I know I've done many awful deeds, and my heart and conscience feel dirty.

Please forgive me! I believe that Jesus Christ died and rose again for my wrongdoing. I accept the free gift of Jesus and ask Him into my heart as my Savior. Amen. (or pray from your heart in your own expressions.)

If this was sincerely prayed from your heart, you are, from this very moment, His child. You have been "born again" (John 3:3), made a "new creation" (2 Corinthians 5:17), and you are totally prepared [you have your passport] to enter into the eternal home with Jesus! [Psalms 23]

If you accepted Jesus Christ as your Savior, you will desire to start your new life. You will want to know how to walk with Him, talk with Him, worship Him, and navigate your life with His peace, love & joy! A true understanding of the gift of Salvation supernaturally leads to a desire to fellowship and walk closer with your Savior (meaning wanting to be like Jesus of Nazareth).

It leads to a heart of thanksgiving and a desire to praise Him. I encourage you to begin your Christian walk today!

Always remember, my friend, that Salvation is based on the merits of Jesus Christ, plus nothing else! Salvation is a gift from God and requires no further action on our part. [Please note, you will still wrestle with sins and temptations in your life, but now you have God's peace and assurance of life eternal and a clean conscience to fight the good fight of faith! (1 Peter 1:3-10)

Marvelously, now begins the process of being a disciple, living a life which brings God glory and pleases Him.

Micah 6:8 NKJV: "He has shown you, O man, what is good; And what does the LORD require of you.... But to do justly (do what is right), To love mercy, (show love and compassion toward your fellow man), And to walk humbly (remember where you came from), with your God?

Lastly, welcome to the family of God!

AUTHOR AND MINISTRY INFORMATION

The author is a pet owner and a graduate of a Bible College who currently works as a consultant in various business sectors. Married to his lovely wife Lili, he has two sons, one with the Lord and the other in college. He has extensively traveled the world, sharing the good news of Jesus Christ domestically and overseas, encouraging people in both home and church settings to make a personal decision to follow Jesus Christ.

It is his desire to encourage men and women of faith to engage in their own individual study of God's word, through a heart that searches diligently into the word of God (2 Tim. 2:15, Acts 17:11). With the ultimate result of a genuine, ongoing relationship with our Lord, to shine forth as he is, with the "light of life!

For further information, speaking schedule, musical ministry, prayer, feel free to contact us at any time at freedomseven@gmx.uk.com

Grace & His peace be with you!
JohnMark Everheart

REFERENCES

Chapter 2

- http://ancienthistory.about.com/od/attilathehun/ig/Attila- the-Hun/Attila-Empire.htm
- The Dogs of War" in the May issue of *National Geographic* magazine.
- "The Dogs of War" in the June issue of *National Geographic* magazine.
- War Dog Memorial Fund Inc. (www.wardogs.org); U.S. Army Quartermaster Museum, Fort Lee, Va.
- U.S. Army Quartermaster Museum, Fort Lee, Va.; United States War Dogs Association,
- http://germanshepherds.awardspace.info/articles/wardogdocument ary/index.php#:~:text=Documentary%20Finally%20Honors%20 War%20Dog%20 Heroes-- Narrated%20by%20Martin,1969%2C%20 and%20America%20is
- %20at%20war%20in%20Vietnam.
- https://www.si.edu/object/nmah_425415
- https://www.atlasobscura.com/places/cher-ami

Chapter 3

- https://biblehub.com/hebrew/5315.htm
- https://biblehub.com/greek/5590.htm
- https://studybible.info/strongs/G5590
- https://www.blueletterbible.org/lang/lexicon
- https://theexplanation.com/soul-nephesh-biblical-hebrew
- https://www.imdb.com/title/tt0413099/
- https://en.wikipedia.org/wiki/Evan_Almighty
- https://www.imdb.com/title/tt1028532/
- https://en.wikipedia.org/wiki/Hachik%C5%8D

Scripture References